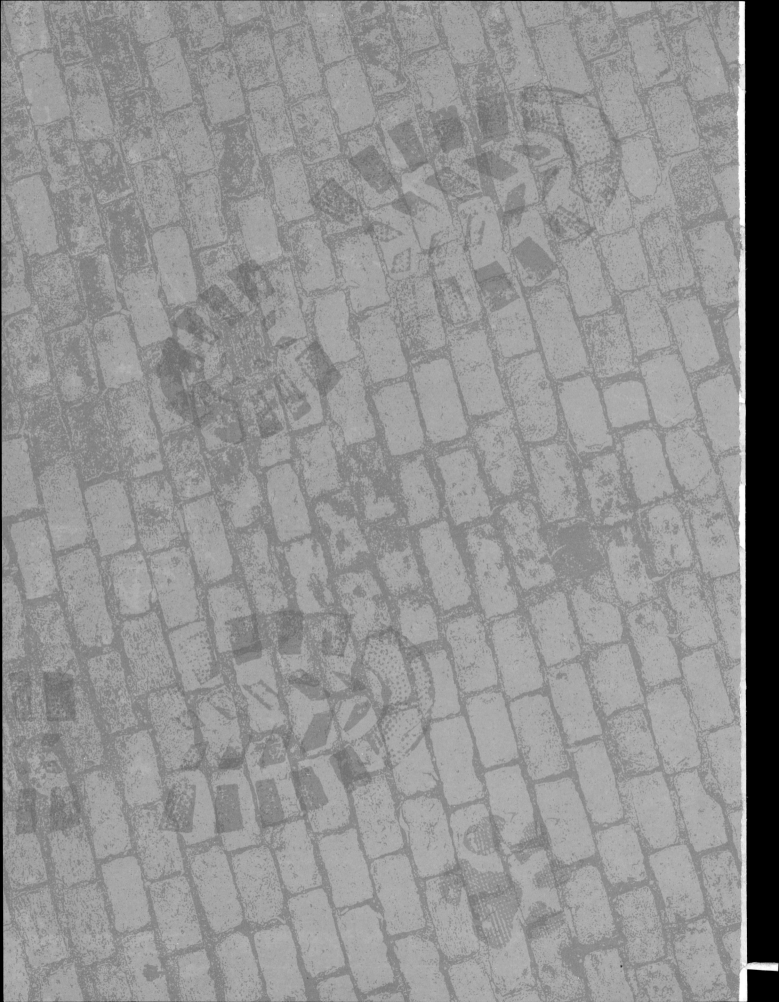

# ROBBERS COPS CRIME

## Roy Apps

WAYLAND
www.waylandbooks.co.uk

# CONTENTS

# BEHAVE YOURSELVES!

When you have a group of people together, somebody has to make sure that everyone behaves themselves. In families, parents or guardians do it; in schools, teachers do it. In the wider community, it's the job of the police to make sure that people stay out of trouble and stick to the law.

The idea of having laws has been around for a very long time. The ancient **Maya civilisation** (who lived in what is now Mexico and Central America) developed a very strict system of law and punishment around 2,000 years ago. Serious crimes were punishable by death, with criminals often being dropped over a cliff! For less serious crimes a person might have had their head shaved.

In ancient Egypt, the police sometimes used monkeys to help them, as this carving shows.

# LAWS – AND OUTLAWS

Romans, Vikings and Normans all invaded Britain and in doing so, they all brought different ideas about crime and punishment …

When the Romans first invaded Britain in 55 BCE, they had no special police force to keep everyone in order. That job was given to the **legionaries** – the Roman soldiers.

In the late ninth century, around half of England was ruled by the Vikings. Under Viking law, all the men who were not slaves gathered together at a meeting called 'the Thing', or Viking assembly, in order to deal with lawbreakers. People found guilty became 'outlaws'. Being an outlaw meant you lost all of your possessions and had to live 'outside the law'. Therefore, anyone could kill an outlaw without being punished.

Viking longships arriving in England

4

When the Normans conquered England in 1066, they brought new laws, called 'forest laws'. If anyone was caught hunting, or even damaging plants and trees in one of the royal forests, they could be fined, or for serious offences, blinded.

In the late fourteenth century, stories spread about a brave and heroic outlaw who lived in Sherwood Forest in Nottinghamshire, England. He was said to steal from the rich and give to the poor. His name, of course, was Robin Hood.

A statue of Robin Hood in Nottingham, England

# MOB RULE AND MAGISTRATES

In 1348, a terrible plague called the Black Death swept through England. It is estimated that by 1350, it had killed around two million people: at least one third of the population. Law and order broke down completely during this time, and many places were ruled by mobs and gangs.

Something had to be done. In 1361, an **Act of Parliament** was passed requiring every county in the land to choose 'good and lawful men' to help restore law and order. They were called 'Justices of the Peace' or **magistrates**.

There are still magistrates working in local courts today. They deal with minor crimes, such as motoring offences. More serious crimes, such as murder and robbery, are dealt with at the **crown courts**.

Victims of the Black Death

An illustration of Ordeal by Water

Before the 1361 Justices Act, one of the ways in which people could be tried for a crime was by 'Ordeal by Water'. The accused were tied up and thrown into a lake or river. If they floated, they were believed to be guilty and executed. If they sank, they were thought to be innocent – which was great as long as someone could get them out of the water before they drowned!

# CAPITAL PUNISHMENT

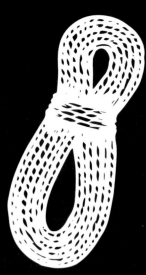

In eighteenth-century England, life for the poor was hard. People would steal food just to keep themselves and their families alive. As crimes such as theft increased, so too, did the severity of the punishments.

In 1723, an Act of Parliament was passed increasing the number of crimes for which a person could be executed. People called it 'the Bloody Code'. Under this law there were 215 crimes that carried the death sentence, such as **poaching** rabbits and stealing food. In fact, someone could have been sentenced to death for stealing anything worth more than five shillings (about £30 in today's money). Until 1868, hangings took place in public. The government thought that this would frighten people into obeying the law.

A prisoner waits to be hanged

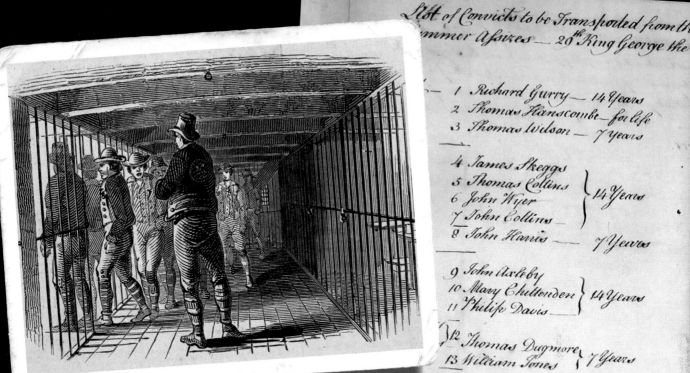

Convicts await transportation

List of Convicts to be Transported from the
Summer Assizes — 29th King George the

1 Richard Gurry — 14 Years
2 Thomas Hanscombe — for life
3 Thomas Wilson — 7 Years

4 James Skeggs
5 Thomas Collins
6 John Wyer                  } 14 Years
7 John Collins
8 John Harris — 7 Years

9 John Axleby
10 Mary Chittenden } 14 Years
11 Philip Davis

12 Thomas Dugmore } 7 Years
13 William Jones

Sussex      14 John Savage   } 14 Years
            15 Samuel Jenner

Surry       16 John Humphreys 14 Yrs
            17 Catherine Fielding
            18 John Cheshyre
            19 Eliz. Wheymark
            20 Danl. Byass
            21 John Same       } 7 Years
            22 Jos: Steele
            23 James Tugman
            24 Willm Coombes
            25 Mary Frivet

are to Certify that Andrew Reed of London Merc
the same Merchant hath Contracted & Given Secur
ation of the 25 Persons above named to be Transported
Essex Kent, Sussex & Surry and the Securities for
hands Dated this Eleventh day of September 1755
of the Reign of King George the Second; Jerom
of the Assizes

RECORD OF
TREASURY
Please to turn over    67

A passenger list shows the ages of some
of the children being transported

Towards the
end of the 1700s, the
number of people being
hanged for such **petty crimes**
was causing public unrest.
It was therefore decided that
people convicted of crimes such
as theft should be shipped to
Britain's new colonies: between
1788 and 1868 more than
160,000 convicts were sent to
Australia. Many of them
were aged between
nine and 14.

# THE BOW STREET RUNNERS

Although hanging got rid of some criminals, it didn't get rid of crime. People were particularly terrified of highwaymen – ruthless thieves on horseback who robbed travellers at gunpoint. Something had to be done …

In 1749, a London magistrate called Henry Fielding set up a small group of men who would investigate crimes, arrest offenders and present evidence at the Old Bailey – London's main criminal court. The government initially gave Henry £200 to help recruit, train and pay his special 'force'. This small group of men became known as the Bow Street Runners (as their headquarters was at Bow Street Magistrates' Court). They travelled all over the country in search of criminals …

A highwayman holds up a stagecoach

When Henry Fielding died in 1754, his half-brother Sir John Fielding, who was also a magistrate, took charge of the Bow Street Runners. Sir John had been blinded in an accident when he was 19. It was said he could recognise some three thousand criminals by the sound of their voices alone.

Henry Fielding

Bow Street Magistrates' Court

# BOBBIES AND PEELERS

In the Scottish city of Glasgow, **watchmen** were once employed to guard the streets at night. They were helped by unpaid **constables**. In 1800, the constables were formed into a paid police force. As well as dealing with crime, they had to sweep the streets and put out fires! Other forces soon followed …

In 1829, the **Home Secretary** of the day, Sir Robert Peel, set up the Metropolitan Police Force in London. There were a thousand officers to begin with. They wore blue coats and top hats, designed to make them look more like ordinary people, rather than soldiers. They each carried a wooden truncheon, a pair of handcuffs and a wooden rattle to raise the alarm. People nicknamed them 'bobbies' or 'peelers' after their founder, Sir Robert Peel. Bobbies had to be aged between 20 and 27, fit, able to read and write, and have no history of wrong-doing.

'Bobbies' outside Enfield Police Station in 1857

In 1798, 31 years before the Metropolitan Police Force was formed, a group of London merchants set up the Marine Police Force to tackle theft and **looting** from ships docked on the River Thames. There are still river police today. They are now part of the Metropolitan Police.

Marine Police in the nineteenth century ...

... and river police at work today

# GETTING AWAY WITH MURDER!

Although the Bow Street Runners and Sir Robert Peel's bobbies both carried out detective work, they weren't trained to deal with serious crime. It was all too easy to get away with murder …

In April 1842, a London police officer was searching some stables for stolen goods, when he made a grisly discovery: the headless body of a woman. He heard a noise behind him, turned around and found himself face-to-face with the murderer. He was so shocked, he didn't know what to do and so the murderer escaped and was on the run for weeks. The case made headlines and the police were mocked for taking so long to catch the criminal, named Daniel Good.

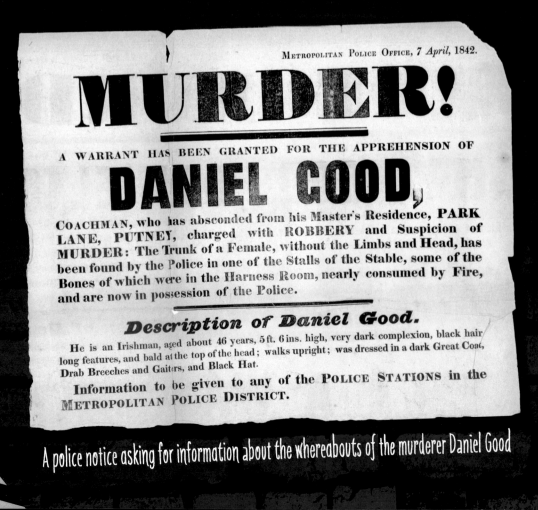

METROPOLITAN POLICE OFFICE, 7 April, 1842.

# MURDER!

A WARRANT HAS BEEN GRANTED FOR THE APPREHENSION OF

## DANIEL GOOD,

COACHMAN, who has absconded from his Master's Residence, PARK LANE, PUTNEY, charged with ROBBERY and Suspicion of MURDER: The Trunk of a Female, without the Limbs and Head, has been found by the Police in one of the Stalls of the Stable, some of the Bones of which were in the Harness Room, nearly consumed by Fire, and are now in possession of the Police.

### Description of Daniel Good.

He is an Irishman, aged about 46 years, 5 ft. 6 ins. high, very dark complexion, black hair, long features, and bald at the top of the head; walks upright; was dressed in a dark Great Coat, Drab Breeches and Gaiters, and Black Hat.

Information to be given to any of the POLICE STATIONS in the METROPOLITAN POLICE DISTRICT.

A police notice asking for information about the whereabouts of the murderer Daniel Good

Shortly after Good's trial and execution, the Metropolitan Police set up a small 'detective force', which in 1878 became the Criminal Investigation Department (CID).

In 1890, the Metropolitan Police Force's headquarters moved to new offices overlooking the River Thames, in London at New Scotland Yard. Everyone called it simply, 'Scotland Yard'. There have been a number of headquarters buildings since then, all of them known as 'Scotland Yard'.

New Scotland Yard in 1895

# SHERLOCK HOLMES LEADS THE WAY!

The most famous detective of all – Sherlock Holmes – is fictional. In the 1890 story, *The Sign of the Four*, Holmes uses fingerprints to help solve the case. It wasn't until 11 years later that detectives from Scotland Yard started using fingerprints to identify criminals.

In 1905, two brothers, Albert and Alfred Stratton, stood accused of murdering a shopkeeper and his wife in south-east London. In court, Detective Inspector Charles Stockley Collins asked the **jury** to compare images of the Strattons' thumbprints taken from the crime scene with prints taken at the police station. He explained to the jury that of the 800,000 fingerprints held by Scotland Yard, he had never found two that matched. The jury saw that the prints were the same. The Strattons were found guilty and hanged – the first murderers to be convicted using fingerprint evidence.

It's not surprising that Sherlock Holmes used scientific methods to catch criminals. The author of the Sherlock Holmes stories, Sir Arthur Conan Doyle, was a doctor and had a keen interest in science. Other scientific methods that can be found in his detective series are the investigation of footprints, handwriting and soil types – all techniques used by real-life detectives.

chest, and then struck me in the
That was in the evening. I had n
for food that Sunday, and
I know Alfred had no
Some neighbours then came
Chapfield and Mrs. Woo
knew as Mrs Bain. The
in the house. They got
water and bathed my eye, a
asked Alfred Stratton to go ou
He went out, and returned abou
twelve. Mrs Chapfield and Mr
Bain were in the room when he ca
home. They went upstairs, and
Alfred and I went to bed.
I think I went to sleep. The
first I remember the following morning
– 27 March – was hearing a tap
at the window. Alfred got out
and spoke to some one outside.

12

Some of the notes made Detective Inspector Charles Stockley Collins during the Stratton case

# FEMALE POLICE OFFICERS

Women were not actively involved in police work until the start of the First World War, when Voluntary Women Patrols (VWPs) were set up in London. More than two thousand women volunteered for this work.

The first-ever female police constable in the UK was Edith Smith. She joined the police force in 1915, in Grantham, Lincolnshire. However, not long after she started, the government issued a ruling saying that women could not be police officers as they were not 'proper persons'! This was because the law barred women from voting and from serving on a **jury** in court.

Edith Smith, the UK's first female police constable

Members of the Metropolitan Women Police Patrol in 1918

In 1918, women over the age of 30 (who had property or were married to someone with property) got the vote and so women gradually became accepted into the country's police force. But even then they weren't allowed to carry truncheons; only umbrellas! Up until the 1980s, female police officers were usually only given tasks that involved domestic disputes or the care of children.

Today there are more than 35,000 female police officers in England and Wales with more than 40 female chief police officers. Women make up around 8 per cent of firearms officers and 45 per cent of specialist crime officers. Specialist crime officers include those whose job it is to protect the Royal Family.

# CALLING ALL CARS!

Responding quickly to a crime has always been an important part of police work. Among the earliest police vehicles were motorbikes. These were given to some of the very first female police officers in 1918.

In the 1920s and '30s, police cars were used to save money. With a car and a radio, one officer could cover a much larger area. But the drivers often weren't very experienced, and there were lots of accidents. So in 1934, the first Metropolitan Police Driving School was set up in Hendon, North London.

*Radio-equipped motorcycle patrol in the 1930s*

Police officers at the Police Driving School with a car and motorcycles, in the 1960s

The Lancashire Crime Patrol scheme inspired one of the most popular British TV police series called *Z-Cars*. Over eight hundred episodes of *Z-Cars* were screened between 1962 and 1978.

In the early 1960s, in an effort to cut crime, the Chief Constable of Lancashire started a new scheme, called 'Crime Patrol'. Instead of one officer patrolling the streets on foot, two officers would drive round in specially modified, high-powered Ford Zephyrs.

# FORENSIC SCIENTISTS

The use of scientific methods to help solve crimes is called forensics. In recent years, new discoveries in biology and chemistry have meant that forensics has become an even more important part of solving crime …

One way in which forensic scientists work is to search for and examine 'trace materials' at a crime scene. Trace materials include blood, hair, fabric fibres, fragments of paint or glass and tyre marks. This evidence can be matched to a suspect, or a suspect's clothes to help solve a crime.

In Britain, collecting forensic evidence from a crime scene is the responsibility of 'Scenes of Crime Officers', or SOCOs. Although SOCOs are employed by the police service, they are not usually police officers. SOCOs are also responsible for taking photographs of a crime scene.

Crime scene investigators collecting fingerprints

DNA profiling – sometimes called DNA fingerprinting – helps forensic scientists to compare the blood, hair or saliva sample found at a crime scene with that of a suspect or victim. If the DNA profiles match, there is only a one-in-a-billion chance that they are from two different people – unless they are identical twins.

*Photographing a crime scene*

23

# COMPUTERS AND CRIME

Sherlock Holmes may only have been a fictional character, but his namesake 'HOLMES' is a vital part of policing today. The twenty-first-century HOLMES is not a detective in a deerstalker hat though, but a powerful computer system!

In 1986, UK police forces began to use an IT system for all major incidents, including serial murders, multi-million-pound **fraud** cases and major disasters. It was called the Home Office Large Major Enquiry System (**HOLMES**). HOLMES helped every police force to share information about incidents and suspects across the UK. A new, modernised system called HOLMES 2 is used today. In any major incident, HOLMES 2 will be set up in a Major Incident Room. The Major Incident Team (MIT) will consist of detectives, crime-scene investigators and staff responsible for operating HOLMES 2.

In recent years, the Internet has been a major help in solving crime. Unfortunately, it has also provided new opportunities for criminals. It is estimated that cybercrime costs the UK more than £30 billion per year. Some cybercrime is aimed at large companies; while some targets individuals, and includes Internet fraud, email scams, computer viruses, hacking and cyberbullying.

Officers using HOLMES 2 in a Major Incident Room

# OUT AND ABOUT

Major incidents are just one part of modern police work.
Most police officers operate in teams that work in a local area.

The area that a police officer patrols is called a beat. Sir Robert Peel's bobbies patrolled on foot. Today, beat officers still patrol on foot, but they also use bicycles, horses, motorbikes and patrol cars – whatever will help them respond quickly to incidents, such as street crimes, burglaries, disturbances and Road Traffic Collisions (RTCs).

A police officer on the beat

Some of the UK's earliest police dogs began working with the North Eastern Railway Police, patrolling the Hull docks in 1908. The dogs' names were Jim, Vic, Mick and Ben. Today, there are around 2,500 dogs employed by police forces across the UK. Specialist Search Dogs (SSDs) are used to sniff out drugs, cash, weapons and explosives. General Purpose Dogs (GPDs) are trained to track and chase criminals, and to search for missing people.

A drug sniffer dog with his handler at Aberdeen airport, Scotland

Every area patrolled by a police force has a Community Policing Team (CPT) that offers advice about keeping yourself and your property safe. You may have officers from a CPT visit your school.

# BEHIND THE SCENES

Most police officers are attached to a local police station. Inside a police station is a front desk, where members of the public can make enquiries, offices and a custody suite.

Look familiar? Yes, that's right, the creators of Doctor Who decided to base the design of the TARDIS on a London police box!

The custody suite is a secure part of the station and is where suspected criminals are taken. It contains cells, and rooms for police to interview suspects or for suspects to talk to solicitors. It is where a suspect's fingerprints, photographs and saliva samples may be taken for police records.

Before mobile phones were invented, 'police boxes' could be found on British street corners. Police officers and members of the public could use these to contact their local station. The boxes were like mini police stations and contained a phone, a first-aid kit, a desk and a stool.

Dagenham Police Station in east London

Police station custody suite and cell

# IF YOU NEED THE POLICE ...

## In an emergency

When you dial 999 you are put through to an operator who will ask which service you need: police, fire, or ambulance. If you ask for the police, you will be put through to the police control room. You should only dial 999 in an emergency, for example, if you witness a road traffic collision or a crime taking place.

## Other police enquiries

It is important not to waste police time, so if you have a non-urgent enquiry you can contact the police by dialling 101. Non-urgent enquiries might be, for example, if you want advice about keeping your property safe or to report information about a crime that has already happened.

# GLOSSARY

**Act of Parliament** A new law or change to an existing law approved by the Houses of Parliament and reigning monarch, such as the Queen.

**capital punishment** When someone is legally killed as punishment for a crime.

**colonies** Countries or areas under political control of another country.

**constable** A police officer of the lowest rank.

**Crown Court** A court of England and Wales that deals with serious criminal cases, such as murder.

**DNA** The substance found in living creatures, which carries genetic information from the parents.

**fraud** Deliberate trickery in order to gain personal advantage or money.

**HOLMES** A powerful computer system that allows police forces to share information across the UK.

**Home Secretary** A senior member of UK government responsible for police, keeping the country safe, immigration and passports.

**jury** A group of people who must decide whether a person is guilty or not guilty, based on facts presented to them in court.

**legionaries** Roman soldiers.

**looting** To steal goods during a war or riot.

**magistrate** A person in charge of a local court, who deals with minor cases and offences, and grants licences.

**Maya civilisation** The ancient people who made their home in an area called Mesoamerica (modern-day Mexico and Central America).

**petty crimes** Amall crimes such as theft or trespassing

**poaching** The illegal hunting of wild animals.

**stagecoach** A large, horse-drawn carriage used to carry passengers between towns.

**watchmen** Men employed to patrol an area, especially at night.

# INDEX

First published in Great Britain in 2017 by Wayland

Copyright © Hodder and Stoughton, 2017

All rights reserved.
ISBN: 978 1 5263 0081 2
10 9 8 7 6 5 4 3 2 1

Printed in China

Wayland
An imprint of
Hachette Children's Group
Part of Hodder & Stoughton
Carmelite House
50 Victoria Embankment
London EC4Y 0DZ

An Hachette UK Company
www.hachette.co.uk
www.hachettechildrens.co.uk

Author: Roy Apps
Editor: Corinne Lucas and Hannah Pang
Designer: Alyssa Peacock
Consultant: Timothy Cross, National Archives

Jacket illustration by Giordano Poloni

The National Archives is the UK government's official archive
containing over 1,000 years of history. They give detailed
guidance to government departments and the public sector on
information management, and advise others about the care
of historical archives. Images reproduced by permission of The
National Archives, London England.

Picture credits:
P3 © Werner Forman/Contributor/Getty images; P4 © Mary
Evans/Interfoto; P6 © Mary Evans Picture Library; P7 ©
Hulton Archive/Getty Images; P8 © Crown Copyright; P9l ©
Crown Copyright; P9r © Crown Copyright; P 10 © Pictorial
Press Ltd/Alamy Stock Photo; P 11l © Hulton Archive/
Handout/Getty Images; P 11r © Culture Club/Contributor/
Getty Images; P 13t © The Keasbury-Gordon Photograph
Archive / Alamy Stock Photo; P 13b © Angelina Dimitrova/
Shutterstock; p16 © Nebojsa S/Shutterstock; p17 © Crown
Copyright; p18 ©Metropolitan Police Authority/Mary Evans;
p21t ©Metropolitan Police Authority/Mary Evans; p21b
© pbpgalleries/Alamy Stock Photo; p22 © Couperfield/
Shutterstock; p23 © Corepics VOF/Shutterstock; p25 © epa
european pressphoto agency b.v. / Alamy Stock Photo; p26
© TTStock/Shutterstock; p27 © Simon Price / Alamy Stock
Photo; p28 © Ints Vikmanis /Shutterstock.com; p29t ©
BasPhoto/Shutterstock; p29b © Mark Bourdillon/Alamy Stock
Photo; p30 © marcyano/Shutterstock.